*For those who are willing
to believe in their dreams
and in themselves,
life is a precious gift
in which anything is possible.*

— Dena Dilaconi

Follow Your Dreams Wherever They Lead You

A Blue Mountain Arts® Collection

Blue Mountain Press™

SPS Studios, Inc., Boulder, Colorado

Library of Congress Catalog Card Number: 2001001040
ISBN: 0-88396-589-5

ACKNOWLEDGMENTS appear on page 64.

Certain trademarks are used under license.

Manufactured in China

First Printing: February 2001

 This book is printed on recycled paper.

This book is printed on fine quality, laid embossed, 80 lb. paper. This paper has been specially produced to be acid free (neutral pH) and contains no groundwood or unbleached pulp. It conforms with all the requirements of the American National Standards Institute, Inc., so as to ensure that this book will last and be enjoyed by future generations.

Library of Congress Cataloging-in-Publication Data

Follow your dreams, wherever they lead you.
        p. cm.
    ISBN 0-88396-589-5
    1. Self-realization—Quotations, maxims, etc. 2. Conduct of life—
Quotations, maxims, etc. 3. Self-realization—Poetry. 4. Conduct of life—
Poetry.
    PN6084.S45 F65 2001
    158.1—dc21

                                                            2001001040
                                                                    CIP

SPS Studios, Inc.

P.O. Box 4549, Boulder, Colorado 80306

Table of Contents

1 Dena DiIaconi

7 Collin McCarty

8 Deanna Beisser

11 Barbara Cage

12 Douglas Richards

15 Susan Polis Schutz

16 Vicki Silvers

19 Dena DiIaconi

20 Leslie Neilson

23 Susan Polis Schutz

24 Douglas Pagels

27 Rosemary DePaolis

28 Donna Gephart

31 Darwin P. Kingsley

31 Elisa Costanza

32 Karen Poynter Taylor

35 Janet A. Sullivan

36 Susan Polis Schutz

39 Melissa Ososki

40 Henry David Thoreau

40 George Bernard Shaw

41 Susan A. J. Lyttek

43 Christian D. Larson

44 Nancye Sims

47 Tim Tweedie

48 Donna Fargo

51 Laine Parsons

52 Nancye Sims

55 D. L. Riepl

56 Susan Polis Schutz

59 Vickie M. Worsham

60 Douglas Pagels

63 Judy LeSage

64 Acknowledgments

"Words of Wisdom"

That Will Keep a Smile on Your Face,
Keep Your Motivation in Place,
and Help Your Dreams Come True

You're good, but you're going to be great ➤ You're the best,
but you're going to get better ➤ Sometimes the paths we
take are long and hard, but remember: those are always the
ones that lead to the most beautiful views ➤ Challenges
come along, inevitably; how you respond to them determines
who you are — deep down inside — and everything you're
going to be ➤ Increase the chances of reaching your goals
by working at them gradually ➤ The very best you can do is
all that is asked of you ➤ Realize that you are capable of
working miracles of your own making ➤ Remember that
opportunities have a reason for knocking on your door, and
the right ones are there for the taking ➤ You don't always
have to win, but you do need to know what it takes to be
a winner ➤ It's up to you to find the key that unlocks the
door to a more fulfilling life ➤ Understand that increased
difficulty brings you nearer to the truth of how to survive
it — and get beyond it ➤ Cross your bridges ➤ Meet your
challenges ➤ Reach out for your dreams, and bring them
closer and closer to your heart ➤ Get rid of the "if only's,"
and get on with whatever you need to do to get things
right ➤ Go after what you want in life, with all the
blessings of all the people who care about you ➤ And find
out what making your wishes come true really feels like ➤

— Collin McCarty

Keep Believing in Yourself and Your Special Dreams

There may be days
when you get up in the morning
and things aren't the way
you had hoped they would be.
That's when you have to tell yourself
that things will get better.
There are times when people
disappoint you and let you down,
but those are the times
when you must remind yourself
to trust your own judgments
and opinions,
to keep your life focused on
believing in yourself
and all that you are capable of.

There will be challenges to face
and changes to make in your life,
and it is up to you to accept them.
Constantly keep yourself headed
in the right direction for you.

It may not be easy at times,
but in those times of struggle
you will find a stronger sense
  of who you are,
and you will also see yourself
developing into the person
you have always wanted to be.

Life is a journey through time,
filled with many choices;
each of us will experience life
in our own special way.
So when the days come
that are filled with frustration
and unexpected responsibilities,
remember to believe in yourself
and all you want your life to be,
because the challenges and changes
will only help you to find
the dreams that you know
are meant to come true for you.

— *Deanna Beisser*

You Can Be or Do Anything!

Believe that you can, and you will. Imagine yourself to be the type of person you want to be, and then be it. You may have to let go of some bad habits and develop some more positive ones, but don't give up — for it is only in trying and persisting that dreams come true.

Expect changes to occur, and realize that the power to make those changes comes from within you. Your thoughts and actions, the way you spend your time, your choices and decisions determine who you are and who you will become.

You are capable and worthy of being and doing anything. You just need the discipline and determination to see it through. It won't come instantly, and you may backslide from time to time, but don't let that deter you. Never give up.

Life is an ever-changing process, and nothing is final. Therefore, each moment and every new day is a chance to begin anew. May all your wishes and dreams come true. They will... if you believe in yourself.

— Barbara Cage

Poems to Help You Be Strong Along the Path of Your Dreams

"Always keep your goodness
and never lose your love.
For then you'll be
rewarded with success
in ways you never dreamed of."

"You can be head and shoulders above the crowd.
You don't have to be a giant to be strong.
Walk tall and be proud. All you have to be...
is someone people look up to."

"In the course of time, you will be reminded
that hard work gets good results and keeping
healthy is essential. Know when to work your mind
and let your body relax, and know when doing just
the opposite makes the most sense. Being able
to handle whatever life brings your way
is not a matter of coincidence."

"You've already got a good idea of what is expected
of you and wished for you. One of the best things
you can accomplish on life's pathway is to be a
walking example of the golden rule. Don't let
anyone fool you into thinking that it is worthless;
it is one of the most valuable things you can do."

"You've got so many possibilities ahead! Don't be too quick to
limit your choices of what to do, because you might limit your
chances of unimagined joys that are waiting just for you."

"You've got a wonderful sense of
humor and a good outlook on life.
Let those qualities help to see you
through when you're deciding where
to go and you're not sure what to do."

"You've got a big heart. Keep it filled with happiness.
You've got a fascinating mind. Keep finding new ways to grow.
Keep yearning. Keep learning. Keep trying. Keep smiling.
And keep remembering that love goes with you...
everywhere you go."

— Douglas Richards

This Life Is Yours

This life is yours
Take the power
to choose what you want to do
and do it well
Take the power
to love what you want in life
and love it honestly
Take the power
to walk in the forest
and be a part of nature
Take the power
to control your own life
No one else can do it for you
Nothing is too good for you
You deserve the best
Take the power to make your life
healthy
exciting
worthwhile
and very happy

— Susan Polis Schutz

Follow Your Destiny
Wherever It Leads You

There comes a time in your life when you realize that if you stand still, you will remain at this point forever. You realize that if you fall and stay down, life will pass you by.

Life's circumstances are not always what you might wish them to be. The pattern of life does not necessarily go as you plan. Beyond any understanding, you may at times be led in different directions that you never imagined, dreamed, or designed. Yet if you had never put any effort into choosing a path or trying to carry out your dream, then perhaps you would have no direction at all.

Rather than wondering about or questioning the direction your life has taken, accept the fact that there is a path before you now. Shake off the "why's" and "what if's," and rid yourself of confusion. Whatever was — is in the past. Whatever is — is what's important. The past is a brief reflection. The future is yet to be realized. Today is here.

Walk your path one step at a time — with courage, faith, and determination. Keep your head up and cast your dreams to the stars. Soon your steps will become firm and your footing will be solid again. A path that you never imagined will become the most comfortable direction you could have ever hoped to follow.

Keep your belief in yourself and walk into your new journey. You will find it magnificent, spectacular, and beyond your wildest imaginings.

— *Vicki Silvers*

Remember that
Anything Is Possible!

Believe in what makes you feel good.
Believe in what makes you happy.
Believe in the dreams you've always wanted to
    come true, and give them every chance to.
Life holds no promises
    as to what will come your way.
You must search for your own ideals
    and work toward reaching them.
Life makes no guarantees
    as to what you'll have.
It just gives you time to make choices
    and to take chances
and to discover whatever secrets
    might come your way.
If you are willing to take the opportunities you
    are given and utilize the abilities you have,
you will constantly fill your life with special
    moments and unforgettable times.
No one knows the mysteries of life
    or its ultimate meaning,
but for those who are willing to believe
    in their dreams and in themselves,
life is a precious gift
    in which anything is possible.

— Dena DiIaconi

Above All Else...

Believe in Yourself

As the dawn of each morning
peers into your life,
there lies a path to follow.
Delicate whispers can be heard
if you listen to the sound of your heart
and the voice that speaks within you.
If you listen closely to your soul,
you will become aware of your dreams
that have yet to unfold.
You will discover that there lies within you
a voice of confidence and strength
that will prompt you to seek a journey
and live a dream.

Within the depths of your mind,
the purpose and direction of your life
can be determined by listening intently
to the knowledge that you already possess.
Your heart, mind, and soul
are the foundation
of your success and happiness.
In the still of each passing moment,
may you come to understand that
you are capable of reaching a higher destiny.
When you come to believe
in all that you are
and all that you can become,
there will be no cause for doubt.
Believe in your heart, for it offers hope.
Believe in your mind, for it offers direction.
Believe in your soul, for it offers strength.
But above all else... believe in yourself.

— Leslie Neilson

People Who Achieve
Their Dreams...

They have confidence in themselves
They have a very strong sense of purpose
They never have excuses
They always strive towards perfection
They never consider the idea of failing
They work extremely hard towards their goals
They know who they are
They understand their weaknesses
    as well as their strong points
They can accept and benefit from criticism
They know when to defend what they are doing
They are creative
They are not afraid to be a little different
They look for innovative solutions
    that will enable them to achieve their dreams

— Susan Polis Schutz

This is how it works.

Each new day is a blank page in the diary of your life. The pen is in your hand, but the lines will not all be written the way you choose; some will come from the world and the circumstances that surround you.

But for the many things that <u>are</u> in your control, there is something special you need to know...

The secret of life is in making your story as beautiful as it can be. Write the diary of your days and fill the pages with words that come from the heart. As the pages take you through time, you will discover paths that add to your happiness and your sorrows, but if you can do these things, there will always be hope in your tomorrows.

Follow your dreams. Work hard. Be kind. This is all anyone could ever ask: Do what you can to make the door open on a day... that is filled with beauty in some special way. Remember: Goodness will be rewarded. Smiles will pay you back. Have fun. Find strength. Be truthful. Have faith. Don't focus on the things you lack.

Realize that people are the treasures in life — and happiness is the real wealth. Have a diary that describes how you did your best, and...

The rest will take care of itself.

— Douglas Pagels

Goals are dreams and wishes
  that are not easily reached.
You have to work hard to
    obtain them,
  never knowing when
    or where
  you will reach your goal.

But keep trying!
Do not give up hope.
And most of all...
    never stop
      believing in yourself.

For within you
there is someone
    special...

someone wonderful
    and successful.
No matter what you achieve,
  as long as you want it
    and it makes you
      happy,

  you are a success.

— Rosemary DePaolis

Ten "Lessons for Life"

1. Your whole life will be a learning and growing experience, whose extent can only be imagined. Life will be your classroom.

2. Don't let negativity get in your way. Keep a positive attitude with you always. Surround yourself with positive people, and turn "I can't" into "I can."

3. Get involved. No matter what you do, throw yourself into it wholeheartedly. The more of yourself you invest, the more you'll reap the benefits.

4. Make time for play. Think back on all the wonderful moments you had, all the laughter and smiles. Know that many more moments of joy await you.

5. Friends and family are most important. During your most difficult moments and exciting triumphs, they stand beside you. Keep them with you always. They will make life's journey much more rich and rewarding, not to mention fun.

6. *Hard work pays off. Your diligent effort has enriched you already. Your good work ethic and determination will bring big rewards for you as you embark on your career.*

7. *The only way to achieve your goals is to create them in the first place. Be sure to think of realistic, short- and long-term goals, then take steady, positive steps toward achieving them.*

8. *Lots of little efforts have a large payoff. No one climbs a mountain in one great leap! It's done one step at a time. You can climb your own personal mountains this way.*

9. *You can finish anything you start. With drive and perseverance, you can fulfill any goal from beginning to end.*

10. *You will not be graded, tested, or quizzed on these lessons. Just keep them in your heart as you continue your exciting journey through life.*

— *Donna Gephart*

*You have powers you never dreamed of.
You can do things you never thought you
could do. There are no limitations in what
you can do except the limitations in your
own mind as to what you cannot do.*
    Don't think you cannot.
        Think you can.

                    — *Darwin P. Kingsley*

*Don't ever give up your dreams...
and never leave them behind.
Find them; make them yours,
and all through your life,
cherish them,
    and never let them go.*

                    — *Elisa Costanza*

Your Dreams
Are Meant to Come True

You can be all the things
you dream of being,
if you're willing to work hard
and if you believe in yourself more.
You have a special understanding of people:
why they do the things they do,
why they hurt, and why they hurt others.
Learn from the mistakes of others —
accept them; forgive them.
Don't use the roles others have had in your life
as excuses for your mistakes.
Take control and live your own life.
Continue the journey you've begun,
which is inside you.
It is the most difficult journey you'll ever make,
but the most rewarding.
Take strength from those you love,
and let those who love you help you.
Open up your heart; put aside your image
    and find your real self.
Keep your pride, but don't live for it.

Believe in your own goodness, and then do good things.
You are capable of them.
Work at being the you that you want to be.
Sacrifice desires of the moment for long-term goals.
The sacrifices will be for your benefit;
you will be proud of yourself.
As you approach life, be thankful
for all the good things that you have.
Be thankful for all the potential that you're blessed with.
Believe in that potential — and use it.
You are a wonderful person, so do wonderful things.
True happiness must come from within you.
You will find happiness
     by letting your conscience guide you —
          listen to it; follow it.
Your conscience is the key to your happiness.
Don't strive to impress others,
     but strive to impress yourself.

Be the person you were meant to be.
Everything else will follow;
     your dreams will come true.

                              — *Karen Poynter Taylor*

Stay Positive
About Your Future

You have so much to offer,
so much to give, and so much
you deserve to receive in return.
Don't ever doubt that.

Know yourself and all your fine
    qualities.
Rejoice in all your marvelous strengths
  · of mind and body.
Be glad for the virtues that are yours,
    and pat yourself on the back for all
    your many admirable achievements.

Keep positive.
Concentrate on that which
    makes you happy,
        and build yourself up.
Stay nimble of heart,
    happy of thought,
    healthy of mind, and
        well in being.

— Janet A. Sullivan

Believe in Your Dreams

Get to know yourself —
what you can do
and what you cannot do —
for only you can make your
life happy

Believe that by working
learning and achieving
you can reach your goals
and be successful

Believe in your own creativity
as a means of expressing
your true feelings

Believe in appreciating life
Be sure to have fun every day
and to enjoy
the beauty in the world

Believe in love
Love your friends
your family
yourself
and your life

Believe in your dreams
and your dreams can become
a reality

— Susan Polis Schutz

*F*ollow your heart;
never surrender your dreams.
Constantly work toward your goals.
Believe in yourself, and always be truthful.
Take time to enjoy life's pleasures.
Keep your mind open to new experiences.
Think before acting,
but don't forget the joys of spontaneity.
Make your own decisions.
Look out for yourself, but remember
that you share this universe with others.
Look for the good in others —
everybody has their own song to sing.
Live each moment to the fullest,
for a moment too soon becomes a memory.
Look for opportunities, not guarantees.
Hope for the best.
Give people a chance to love you,
for that is how you learn to love.
Live your life for yourself,
but always be considerate of others.
Believe in tomorrow, for it holds the key
to your dreams.

— Melissa Ososki

If one advances confidently in
the direction of his dreams,
and endeavors to live the life
which he has imagined,
he will meet with a success
unexpected in common hours.

— Henry David Thoreau

The people who get on in this
world are the people who get up
and look for the circumstances
they want, and, if they can't
find them, make them.

— George Bernard Shaw

Let Your Dreams Take You Wherever You Want to Go

When the road curves
to lead you into
    new discoveries...
let it take you.
When the wind pulls
    under your wings
and urges you on
    to greater heights...
        let it take you.
When the page you're on
    builds suspense,
        turn it —
for it will end happily.
Let it take you there.
The journey of life
    has no blueprints.
You find it as you grow
through prayer, joy,
pain, and love.
Keep moving on your path,
keep learning and trying
for the good and the best —
and it will take you there.

— Susan A. J. Lyttek

Promise Yourself

Promise yourself to be so strong that nothing can disturb your peace of mind. To talk health, happiness, and prosperity to every person you meet. To make all your friends feel that there is something in them. To look at the sunny side of everything and make your optimism come true. To think only of the best, to work only for the best, and expect only the best. To be just as enthusiastic about the success of others as you are about your own. To forget the mistakes of the past and press on to the greater achievements of the future. To wear a cheerful countenance at all times and give every living creature you meet a smile. To give so much time to the improvement of yourself that you have no time to criticize others. To be too large for worry, too noble for anger, too strong for fear, and too happy to permit the presence of trouble.

— *Christian D. Larson*

Always Hope for the Best

Hope gives you the strength to keep going
when you feel like giving up.
Don't ever quit believing in yourself.
As long as you believe you can,
you will have a reason for trying.
Don't let anyone hold
your happiness in their hands;
hold it in yours,
so it will always be within your reach.
Don't measure success or failure
by material wealth, but by how you feel;
our feelings determine the richness of our lives.
Don't let bad moments overcome you;
be patient, and they will pass.
Don't hesitate to reach out for help;
we all need it from time to time.
Don't run away from love, but toward love,
because it is our deepest joy.

Don't wait for what you want to come to you;
go after it with all that you are,
knowing that life will meet you halfway.
Don't feel like you've lost
when plans and dreams fall short of your hopes.
Anytime you learn something new
about yourself or about life,
you have progressed.
Don't do anything that takes away
from your self-respect;
feeling good about yourself
is essential to feeling good about life.
Don't ever forget how to laugh
or be too proud to cry.
It is by doing both that we live life to its fullest.

— Nancye Sims

What Does It Mean
to Succeed?

Most people see success as being rich and famous or powerful and influential. Others see it as being at the top of their profession and standing out from the rest.

The wise see success in a more personal way; they see it as achieving the goals they have set for themselves, and then feeling pride and satisfaction in their accomplishments. True success is felt in the heart, not measured by money and power.

So be true to yourself and achieve the goals you set. For success is reaching those goals and feeling proud of what you have accomplished.

— Tim Tweedie

Reach for the Stars, Go for Your Dreams!

There are rainbows and pots of gold waiting for you over the horizon, surprises and gifts and wonders just around every corner. Look forward to them. Love them. Catch these pieces of life as they come, and hold them close to you. Savor every moment, every triumph, and even every failure. Don't be afraid to be too passionate to enjoy the ride, chase every quest, and praise every hint of answers to your questions. Dream big. Work hard. Enjoy your play time. Deal with all the challenges in life like the true champ you are. You may not always get what you want, but you're never a failure if you give it your all and do the best you can.

*You don't have to be perfect or the smartest
person in the world to dream. You don't
have to have all the answers or know
everything to make your dream come true.
Dreams are free, but they belong to the
dreamer who'll take a chance.*

*So let your imagination take you to that
perfect place where there is nothing to
be afraid of and you can have anything
you want. Prepare yourself. Knock on the
door of opportunity, and be ready when
it answers. Celebrate all the possibilities.
Your future is full of hope and happy times,
fantasies, and lessons to learn. Learn them
well. Enjoy each one. Be good. Believe in
miracles. Believe that all things are possible.
Love and allow yourself to be loved. Reach
for the stars and go for your dreams.*

— *Donna Fargo*

Don't Ever Stop Dreaming
Your Dreams

Don't ever try to understand everything —
some things will just never make sense.
Don't ever be reluctant
    to show your feelings —
    when you're happy, give in to it!
    When you're not, live with it.
Don't ever be afraid to try to
    make things better —
    you might be surprised at the results.
Don't ever take the weight of the world
    on your shoulders.
Don't ever feel threatened by the future —
    take life one day at a time.
Don't ever feel guilty about the past —
    what's done is done. Learn from any
    mistakes you might have made.
Don't ever feel that you are alone —
    there is always somebody there for you
    to reach out to.
Don't ever forget that you can achieve
    so many of the things you can imagine —
    imagine that! It's not as hard as it seems.
Don't ever stop loving,
    don't ever stop believing,
        don't ever stop dreaming your dreams.

— Laine Parsons

51

Winners Are
People like You

Winners take chances.
Like everyone else, they fear failing,
but they refuse to let fear control them.
Winners don't give up.
When life gets rough, they hang in
until the going gets better.
Winners are flexible.
They realize there is more than one way
and are willing to try others.
Winners know they are not perfect.
They respect their weaknesses
while making the most of their strengths.
Winners fall, but they don't stay down.
They stubbornly refuse to let a fall
    keep them from climbing.
Winners don't blame
    fate for their failures
nor luck for their successes.

Winners accept responsibility
 for their lives.
Winners are positive thinkers
who see good in all things.
From the ordinary, they make
 the extraordinary.
Winners believe in the path they
 have chosen
even when it's hard,
even when others can't see
 where they are going.
Winners are patient.
They know a goal is only as worthy
as the effort that's required to achieve it.
Winners are people like you.
They make this world a
better place to be.

— Nancye Sims

Carry with You These Gifts of the Heart

Trust... that whatever happens,
there is someone who will
understand.
Honesty... the feeling that you
never need to hold back.
Peace... in being accepted for
who you really are.
Beauty... in outlook
more than appearance.
Freedom... to be yourself,
to change, and to grow.
Joy... in every day, in every memory,
and in your hopes for
the future.
Love... to last a lifetime,
and perhaps beyond.

— D. L. Riepl

Always Create Your Own Dreams and Live Your Life to the Fullest

Dreams can come true
if you take the time to
think about what you want in life
Get to know yourself
Find out who you are
Choose your goals carefully
Be honest with yourself
Always believe in yourself
Find many interests and pursue them
Find out what is important to you
Find out what you are good at
Don't be afraid to make mistakes
Work hard to achieve successes
When things are not going right
don't give up — just try harder
Find courage inside of you to remain strong

Give yourself freedom to try out new things
Don't be so set in your ways that you
    can't grow
Always act in an ethical way
Laugh and have a good time
Form relationships with people you respect
Treat others as you want them to treat you
Be honest with people
Accept the truth
Speak the truth
Open yourself up to love
Don't be afraid to love
Remain close to your family
Take part in the beauty of nature
Be appreciative of all that you have
Help those less fortunate than you
Try to make other lives happy
Work towards peace in the world
Live life to the fullest
Create your own dreams
and your dreams will become a reality

— *Susan Polis Schutz*

Believe in Miracles!

Love your life.
Believe in your own power,
  your own potential,
    and your own innate goodness.
Every morning, wake with the awe
  of just being alive.
Each day, discover the magnificent,
  awesome beauty in the world.
Explore and embrace life in yourself
  and in everyone you see each day.
Reach within to find your own specialness.
Amaze yourself,
  and rouse those around you
    to the potential of each new day.
Don't be afraid to admit
  that you are less than perfect;
    this is the essence of your humanity.
Let those who love you help you.
Trust enough to be able to take.
Look with hope to the horizon of today,
  for today is all we truly have.
Live this day well.
Let a little sunshine out as well as in.
Create your own rainbows.
Be open to all your possibilities;
  possibilities can be miracles.
Always believe in miracles!

— *Vickie M. Worsham*

You're a Very Special Person, and You Can Achieve Any Dream

Carry the sun inside you,
and reach out for the dreams
that guide you. You have
everything you need to take
you where you want to go.
You have abilities and talents
and attributes that belong to
  you alone, and you have
    what it takes to make
      your path of success…
        lead to happiness.
You're a very special person.
You have qualities that get better
  every day!
You have the courage and strength
  to see things through.
You have smiles that will serve
  as your guides.

You have a light that will shine in you
  'til the end of time.
You have known the truth of yesterday,
  and you have an inner map that will
  lead the way to a very beautiful
  tomorrow.
You have gifts that have never even been
  opened and personal journeys waiting
  to be explored. You have <u>so</u> <u>much</u> going
  for you.
You are a special person, and you have a
  future that is in the best of hands.
  And you need to remember: If you have
  plans you want to act on and dreams
  you've always wanted to come true…

    You have what it takes, because…
    You
        have
            you.

                                    — Douglas Pagels

May You Never Lose Sight of Your Dreams

In life, there will always be
many paths to follow;
may you always choose the right one.
If you give a part of yourself to life,
the part you receive back
will be so much greater.
Never regret the past,
but learn by it.
Never lose sight of your dreams;
a person who can dream
will always have hope.
Believe in yourself;
if you do, everyone else will.
You have the ability
to accomplish anything,
but never do it at
someone else's expense.
If you can go through life
loving others,
you will have achieved
the greatest success of all.

— Judy LeSage

ACKNOWLEDGMENTS

We gratefully acknowledge the permission granted by the following authors and authors' representatives to reprint their works.

Susan Polis Schutz for "This Life Is Yours," "Believe in Your Dreams," "People Who Achieve Their Dreams...," and "Always Create Your Own Dreams and Live Your Life to the Fullest." Copyright © 1978 by Continental Publications; Copyright © 1984, 1986, 1989 by Stephen Schutz and Susan Polis Schutz. All rights reserved.

Leslie Neilson for "Above All Else... Believe in Yourself." Copyright © 2001 by Leslie Neilson. All rights reserved.

PrimaDonna Entertainment Corp. for "Reach for the Stars, Go for Your Dreams!" by Donna Fargo. Copyright © 2001 by PrimaDonna Entertainment Corp. All rights reserved.

A careful effort has been made to trace the ownership of poems and excerpts used in this anthology in order to obtain permission to reprint copyrighted materials and give proper credit to the copyright owners. If any error or omission has occurred, it is completely inadvertent, and we would like to make corrections in future editions provided that written notification is made to the publisher:

SPS STUDIOS, INC.
P.O. Box 4549, Boulder, Colorado 80306.